This Way to School

Contents

At the Start

This girl lives in the yellow house on Market Street.

Her friend lives across the street
in the blue house.

They meet in front of the market to walk to school together.

They go the same way
every day.

On the Way

This is a map of the way the children go to school.

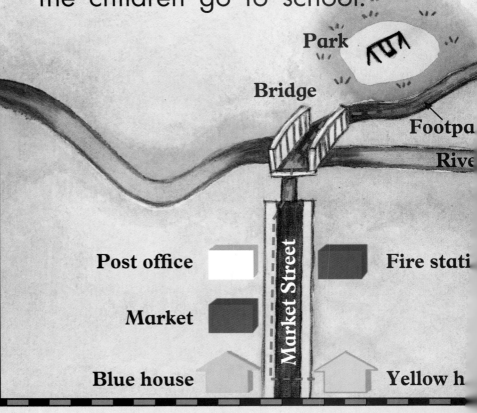

Park

Bridge

Footpa

Rive

Post office

Fire stati

Market

Market Street

Blue house

Yellow h

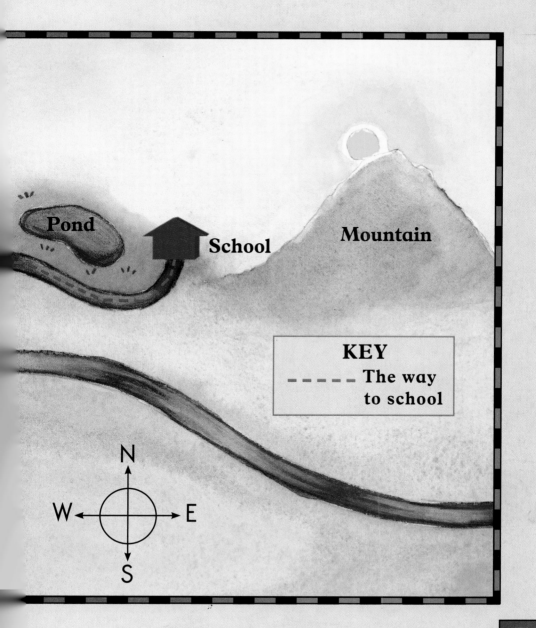

Pond

School

Mountain

KEY

- - - - - The way to school

N
W E
S

They go straight
on Market Street.
The post office is on the left,
near the river.

The fire station is across the street
on the right.
They always wave
to the firefighters.

They stop on the bridge
that goes across the river.

They watch the sun
as it comes up over the mountain.
That direction is east.

The park is past the bridge.
Today they stop to play.

Then they run by the pond
and turn at the front of the school.

At School

The children see their principal in front of the school.
They watch as the flag goes up.

They hurry to class.
Another day of school
is about to start.

Index